A MYSTIC GUIDE TO SPIRITUAL EVOLUTION

A PICTORIAL AND ORAL GUIDE TO EVOLVING AN INDIVIDUAL'S SPIRITUAL CONSCIOUSNESS

WILLIAM J. PARDUE

ISBN   978-1-953821-62-1 Ebook
ISBN   978-1-953821-61-4 Paperback

The EC Publishing LLC books may be ordered through booksellers or by contacting:

EC Publishing LLC
116 South Magnolia Ave.
Suite 3, Unit F
Ocala, FL 34471, USA
Direct Line: +1 (352) 644-6538
Fax: +1 (800) 483-1813
http://www.ecpublishingllc.com/

Ordering Information:
Quantity sales. Special discounts are available on quantity purchases by corporations, associations, and others. For details, contact the publisher at the address above.

Printed in the United States of America

There are infinite levels of consciousness from that of the rock to that of the prophet and beyond. Mankind has floundered in a primal state of consciousness since the earliest man walked the earth and it is that same consciousness which continues to wreak havoc on the Earth and all living forms. Among the contents of this primal consciousness is an antiquated and malignant concept of God. It is a concept that breeds hatred, envy, separatism, materialism and confusion all in the name of righteousness of a God that condemns evil and embraces and rewards all that is good. The obvious flaw becomes defining what is good and what is not and what is God and what is not.

A concept which pits man against man against woman against anything that does not agree with it is destructive not constructive. It is now and always has been the cancer of thought which creates all of our problems and solves none of them. Instead of approaching our problems from within we choose to see their source from without and then attack and eliminate that outside source. The problem with that approach is that once we destroy or eliminate one problem on the outside another automatically takes its place and a new enemy with a new name must be destroyed. When your car runs out of gas you cannot make it go again by replacing the battery. Unless the source of the cancer is addressed the cancer will continue to spread. Our current state of primitive consciousness, which defines our reality and therefore determines our responses to it, is broken, antiquated and lethal to our human family.

There is an entry way to a level of consciousness, within the center of each one of us, where we all simultaneously coexist, where we all can share one common consciousness, which is often referred to as God consciousness or Cosmic Consciousness. This state of consciousness is described as the all-encompassing, omnipresent, omnipotent and omniscient source of all creation. You will not find access to it anywhere or in anything outside of yourself yet it exists everywhere and in everything. Our individual access to It is at the very center of our beings and each one of us must access it ourselves and only then will we be able to experience the presence of God in our lives, the positive effects of a heightened state of consciousness. After all we are, allegedly, the most intelligent of species and are therefore obligated to use that intelligence to evolve physically, mentally and spiritually. As a species we determine the future of this planet by the thoughts in our minds, the limitations of our consciousness.

This pictorial guide is meant to illuminate
the contours of the emotions, feelings and thoughts that inhabit that heightened
state of consciousness. It is the beginning of the journey into the "Light".

The closer we look at ourselves the closer we will look
at the world and the more we will see. The more we see the wiser we will become. Expand
your consciousness beyond your five senses and awaken to the world of your eternal Spirit.

When climbing the ladder of spiritual evolution
there will be a step called "helping others". That step is essential to the perfection
of the spirit for which we are all capable. Skipping it is not an option

When you can maintain equanimity of spirit even
in the jaws of death you have the key to a successful ascent
of the ladder of spiritual evolution.

Do not allow fear to control your life. It creates only
anxiety and imbalance. Allow God, your cosmic consciousness, to
direct your every step and give you the gift of fearlessness

"WHO" WE ARE IS CHANGING FROM MOMENT TO MOMENT
UNTIL THE "WHO" THAT WE ARE CEASES TO EXIST

THE "WHAT" THAT WE ARE IS ETERNAL AND NEVER
CHANGING. IT IS IDENTICAL FOR ALL OF US.

Look for the invisible, listen for the silence, and
feel the untouchable. Discover what you are.

© 2011 Chris Fallows
www.apexpredators.com

Divine Intervention is a purely subjective phenomenon and as such it is beyond the reach of objective tests. You know it when you experience it.

LOVE,

Feel it, Be it, Allow it to have unrestricted access to your life and
feel the transformation of life into all things good

The secret of keeping your balance in life.

All your sensory control information must be tuned to the dynamics of the rope.

Your attention must not be distracted from the high wire which is your
life. Allowing your awareness to wander away from your destiny only to
spend it on irrelevant trivia is a failure to evolve your consciousness to the
highest levels possible. Your fate is in your hands. Pay attention

The "feeling" which we call "love" is a necessary prerequisite to an expansion of consciousness. The more of that feeling you allow the more expansive will be your consciousness.

If we can't love each other, who will love us? Allow yourself to fully experience the feeling which we call love.

HOW DIFFERENT ARE WE REALLY?

See the trust, feel the life in a common heartbeat,
know the inspiration of innocence, appreciate the beauty of contrast accentuating the
sameness, focus your awareness on the manifestation of infinite possibilities made
possible by Cosmic Consciousness. Choose to evolve, move beyond black and white

Moving beyond the limits of your personal consciousness and thereby accessing God consciousness requires conscious acts of "bursting the bubble of your current self". Discover your own limits and dare to move beyond them. Evolve

Dare to believe that your potential, your best self, exists beyond
your fears. Deny fear any foothold in your life.

It only has the life which you give it, withdraw your
attention from fear and it ceases to exist.

We all have our own particular limitations which can cause us problems in life. It is only when we acknowledge the problem that we can transcend it. If you feel like a giraffe up a tree, own the feeling and then move beyond it.

Close your eyes, open your inner eye, be silent and know the beauty of the divine spirit that resides within, that is closer than the end of your nose. Allow it to teach you.

The most poignant fact about enlightenment is that you already have access
to everything you need to be enlightened. There is nothing else you need from
anyone or anything. Turn your attention from the outside to the inside.

Has anyone ever told you 'you're too nice'? That's because you just might be! Don't take it the wrong way, kindness is sorely lacking in the world and no act of kindness, however big or small, is ever wasted. But sometimes you have to stick up for yourself and not let others take you for granted! Just find that happy balance between your kind heart and a stern hand. Use your kindness to help and teach others and you will be just fine!

There are things that you see but do not believe, there are other things which you do not see but which you do believe. The ability to see (become aware of) "things" is controlled by the mind (consciousness) and not the eye. The more evolved your consciousness is the more you are aware of, both seen and unseen. Mankind's evolutionary goal is "cosmic consciousness" and beyond. Allow yourself to evolve.

Evil never dies you just make it irrelevant. Choose "Good" and evolve.

Eggs flash as they meet sperm enzyme, capturing the moment that
life begins CREDIT: NORTHWESTERN UNIVERSITY

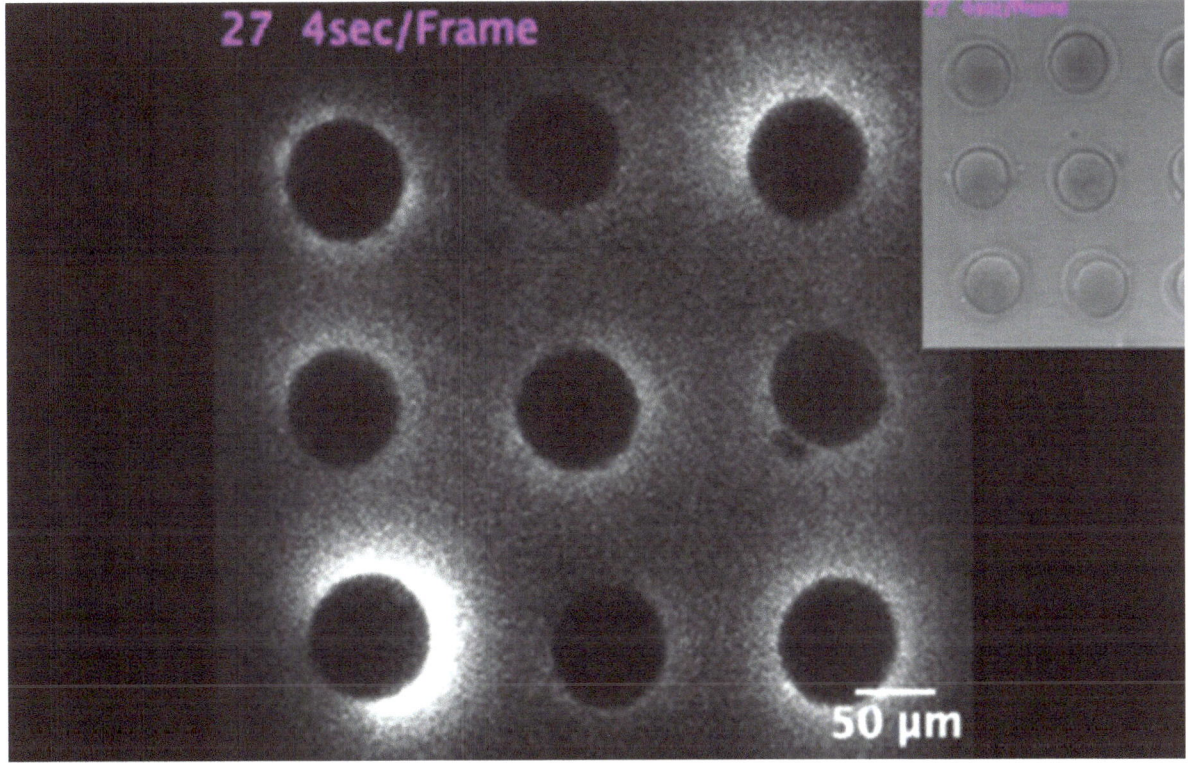

The Buddha was the Buddha before he was born.

Who were you?

You were then and you are now and ever will be a "child of the light"

We are all sitting on the mountaintop believing that the mountain, if it truly exists, is in some faraway and hidden location only accessible to a few chosen ones who have deciphered some mysterious code and yet the portal to the divine is now and always has been and always will be within us. It sits silently waiting for us to acknowledge the "light".

Life is ever changing, passing before our eyes, unstoppable. We either understand that or we desperately take action which we believe will freeze the flow of life. There is no thought, no possession no person that can stop the movement of life. Jump in.

The defining characteristic of a Mystic who succeeds in attaining access to "Cosmic Consciousness" is an unwavering determination driven by an unquenchable desire focused like a laser on the single goal to become one with that presence which we call God.

There is nothing that will make you laugh harder than being in the river playing your flute for your favorite rooster and having it sing along. Laughter is the greatest gift of a joyous God

Success in life requires the same elements as success in the fighting arts. It is not how hard you are thrown or knocked down that count: it is how well you "roll" or absorb and dissipate the energy from the throw that determines your ultimate success in both the material and spiritual worlds.

Fear is a thief which we let into our hearts and our minds. It robs us of our ability to be free, to be daring, to be different, to be happy. It invades our soul and steals from us the glorious destiny which abides within. It is an ominous cancer which cripples our spirit with anxiety and worry. Deny fear. Choose to be courageous and to manifest your dreams.

Raw power which is unleashed causes only destruction. Power is energy and energy is what the human body is composed of, what it needs to survive. We are capable of mining vast reserves of energy but when our limits of control over that energy are exhausted it becomes destructive of our lives and those around us and ultimately the world at large. Learn to control the manifestations of that energy in your desires, emotions and your thoughts. Evolve

KOO KOO THE BIRD GIRL

Look at me and then tell me what you see
Do you see the bonfire of unconditional love that blazes inside, can you see my soul or
Do you see what you do not understand, something that you fear and that upsets you
The choice is yours. Choose for yourself but always be aware of what you are choosing.
One's destiny is paved with the consequences of your choices Choose wisely, Evolve

Be good and all things good will be yours, Be understanding and you will be understood, Be loving and love will find you. Live enlightened. Evolve

Know that it is those silent stirrings within us which we call unconscious that determine the quality and character of life which we live on the conscious plane. Only with a conscious awakening of the unconscious, eternal forces within us can we evolve. Turn inward and meet the divine.

Those who are strong enough to bend their wills gracefully to benefit others, to lower
themselves effortlessly to serve others, have little to fear from the fierce currents
and turmoil of life. They will be tested true, but they will survive and flourish. Eknath Easwaran.

The Mystic Path leads to the crown jewel of human
consciousness; a direct experience of God

An enlightened state of consciousness is best described as
the place where supreme achievement

And complete humility becomes one.

Your home is waiting patiently for you within for we are all prodigal
children destined to return after a long journey

Once enlightened, the Buddha had a good laugh on himself. How silly I have been he thought and the more he thought about it the harder he laughed.

Even a dog can be self- satisfied to the point
of arrogance. Only a man can find humor in his own pretensions but he must
first rise above them and see them for what they are. Have a good laugh.
EVOLVE

The evolution of human consciousness is achieved one person at a time. In reality it is accomplished by cultivating an ever increasing sensitivity to an awareness of occurrences in the spiritual or fourth dimension. The denial of this dimension is posited only by those who have been unable to discern its existence. The three dimensions of man limit his consciousness to only those realities which can be witnessed through the 5 senses. The doorway to fourth dimensional consciousness is deep inside the silence of your soul. Find it and enter the cosmos of the glory that is the infinite and eternal life force, the "Light" within.

Remember that brash baby confidence that you had? When you are feeling particularly low pull it out of your memory bank and have a good laugh. Resurrect the divinity of the child within.

When the forest king can laugh at how odd yet beautiful he can be at the same time; then why can't we laugh at how ridiculous and sublime we can appear in the same moment? Smile like the king and be free.

If your consciousness does not include a concept of a higher power which will protect you from even the biggest storms in your life then perhaps you should consider expanding your concept. Choose to Evolve

Consider the possibility that your concept of god is too small. Of course there is always the thought that any concept or idea of god is too small unless it encompasses all things, all the time, without exception. If your god is not all powerful, all knowing and ever present everywhere then it fails the god test.

When we are unable to feel love and compassion towards those who are in the most need of it, what does that mean? Do we expect something in return and if they have nothing to offer we have nothing to give. Open mind/Open heart.

When we allow ourselves to exist truly and fully, we sting the world
with our vision and challenge it with our own ways of being.

THOMAS MOORE

If your consciousness does not include a concept of a higher power
which will protect you from even the biggest storms in your life then
perhaps you should consider getting a bigger umbrella.

Choose to Evolve your consciousness

The divine spirit within man is indomitable and eternal
Man's body is fragile and temporal
Ride the wave of the divine spirit into an eternity of pure bliss
Enter the "Light" and Evolve

Rest in the rhythm of the "divine spirit" which is life itself

There is no one "thing" that has the power to irritate you without your consent and cooperation. Withhold your consent and refuse to cooperate. Evolve

If you encounter something in life which you cannot find any love in your heart for, you have to ask why. When you discover the answer to that "why" you will discover your own limitations for loving. You then choose to keep your heart closed or open it even wider. Our obligation to God, to the Universe that gave us life, is to spread love unconditionally.

When you meet someone new and you think there is something odd about them consider that they probably think there is something odd about you. Do not forget we are all riding in the same boat down the same stream of life at the same time.

The impulse to help others in life springs from the divinity within you. Any expression of our own divinity always makes the world a better place. Manifest all that is good.

Real love can be shared despite differences. Don't hesitate to
show your love. It is a healing balm for all of us.

A cat wearing a cat mask is only pretending to be a cat it is not being a cat.

The evolution of human consciousness is achieved one person at a time. In reality it is accomplished by cultivating an ever increasing sensitivity to an awareness of occurrences in the spiritual or fourth dimension. The denial of this dimension is posited only by those who have been unable to discern its existence. The three dimensions of man limit his consciousness to only those realities which can be witnessed through the 5 senses. The doorway to fourth dimensional consciousness is deep inside the silence of your soul. Find it and enter the cosmos of the glory that is the infinite and eternal life force. Choose to enter the "Light"

Teased hair is one thing, harassed hair another. Balancing a bundle of hemp gives you this stylish Italian look, too.

Where does the past go? Where does the future come from? Where is the present?

DARKNESS IS MERELY THE ABSENCE OF "LIGHT"

OPEN YOUR HEART, OPEN YOUR MIND, AND OPEN THE DOOR TO
THE LIGHT OF DIVINE CONSCIOUSNESS. EVOLVE

IF YOU CAN'T EXPLAIN IT SIMPLY, YOU SIMPLY DO NOT UNDERSTAND IT WELL ENOUGH

ALBERT EINSTEIN

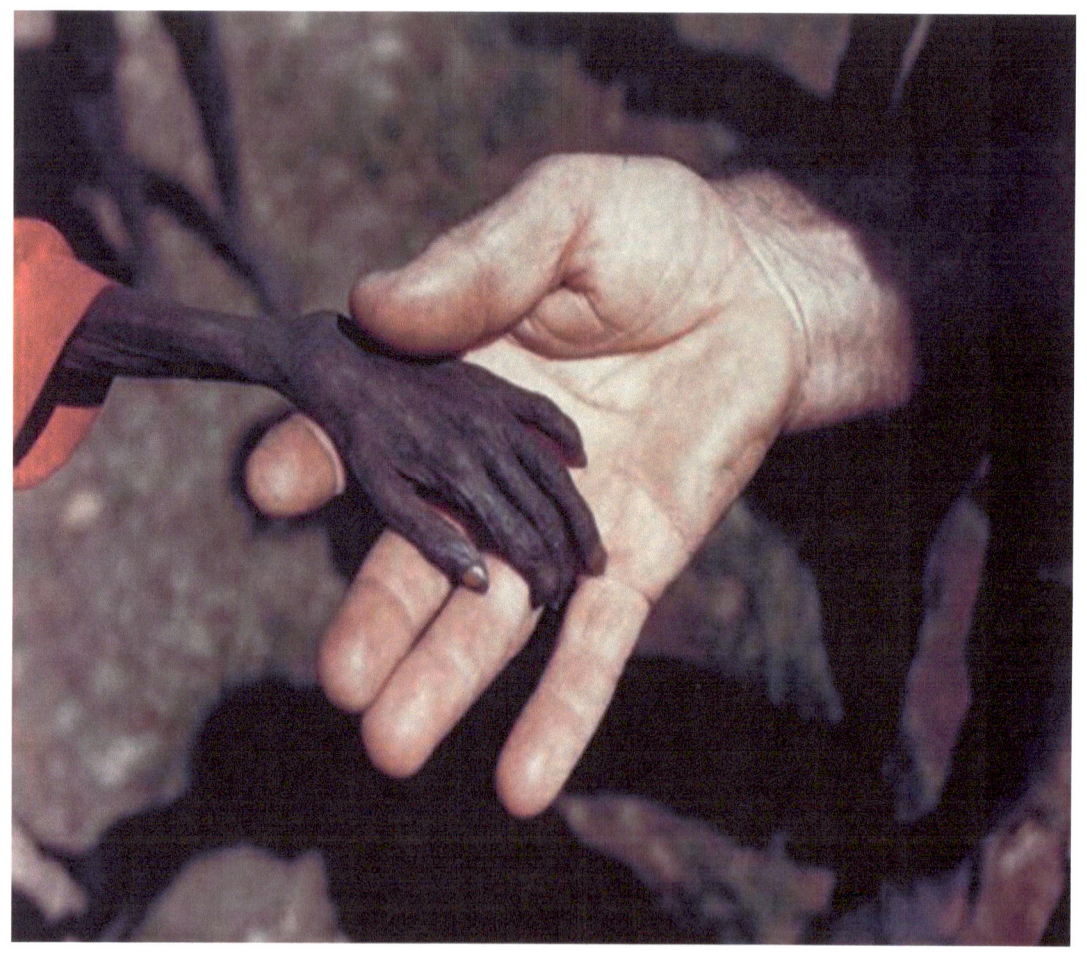

The only color that truly matters is the color of your soul

HOW DO YOU PASS THROUGH THE NARROW GATE TO ATTAIN
A SPIRITUAL LEVEL OF CONSCIOUSNESS?

Abandon all things "self" for the love of the mother ship, the eternal life force, God.

LOOK WITHIN THEN "BE STILL" AND KNOW WHAT GOD IS.

When the Universe asks you "What time is it?" and you are unable to answer, you must then turn to the Universe for that answer. The answer to that question for the seeker is always;

It is time to come home

Move into the "Light"

We are all sitting on the mountaintop believing that the mountain, if it truly exists, is in some faraway and hidden location only accessible to a few chosen ones who have deciphered some mysterious code.

The most poignant fact about enlightenment is that you already have access to everything you need to be enlightened. There is nothing else you need from anyone or anything. Turn your attention from the outside to the inside. Find your light.

Make your life a manifestation and
celebration of all things good

A tree by its very nature provides shade freely and
indiscriminately to all in need without thought of gain.
The human heart by its very nature generates love which is
meant to be freely and indiscriminately available to all in need without
thought of gain. Allow your heart to do what it is meant to do.

MOVE BEYOND YOUR LIMITED SENSE OF SELF BY
WASHING AWAY THE VAGARIES AND LIMITATIONS OF "SELF" WITH
THE DIVINITY AND CLARITY OF YOUR INNER SPIRIT

You can sense the larger part of yourself, your divine self, but
you must look beyond the obvious to find it

Move from the darkness to the light

We must travel within ourselves below the surface of our senses to a place within where you cannot see, hear, taste, feel or think. It is in that place where you will find the healing, the love, and the eternal divinity

FIND YOUR LIGHT AND EVOLVE

If not now when?
Discover your divinity

EVOLVE

WILL YOU EVER HAVE ENOUGH?

What is it about you that attracts other people? Is it your smile, the way you look, who you are and what you have? We are under the false belief that these are the reasons why. The truth is that we are attracted to others who are on the same mental and spiritual wavelength. It is not the visible that brings us together it is the invisible

Do our pets love us more than we love them? I think both humans and our most loyal friends, our pets, are capable of equal amounts of love. The only difference is that an animal is possessed by love and gives itself over to the feeling completely. Other than the truly young and young at heart, humans question love and intentionally limit its power over them.

There is a divine light, a light of life that cares for us, guides us and is always there for us. Our job is to become aware of it and let it shine through us. Live a loving life and reap the rewards!

In the final chapter of your life are you going to wonder how things got so sad, so depressing or are you going to look back with the trained eye of wisdom and experience and know that you lived the best life that you could and you are glad for it. Need a Change, Yes, but when do I have time for it? If not now, when? Time is wasting get on with it!

Have you ever felt like you were lost in the Desert and there was nothing to guide you to your destination? In times like those find a quiet place to sit, with no distractions, and wait for the divine spirit to guide you. It will let you know the right direction you just need to listen for and feel the presence of the divine within and become aware of what direction it wants you to take.

One indication of your level of spiritual awareness is
your response to those in need. If compassion and sincere empathy are
part of your consciousness then you are on the right path. If, however,
criticism and disdain arises then you need a new roadmap.

APOLOGIA

I hope that these photos and words have perhaps captured your attention for a few minutes; long enough perhaps to make you want to know more, to experience the living God. If they have not then I apologize for my impertinence in believing that they may have done just that. However for those of you for whom a chord may have been struck and thought may have manifested as a seed; know that there is indeed within each of us a place of enlightenment, both silent and mysterious where our divinity resides. Find that light and you have found the doorway to our spiritual inheritance which is manifested as eternal bliss, everyday happiness and boundless love.

OPEN HEART/OPEN MIND

William J. Pardue

DEDICATION

This book is dedicated to the Light of Consciousness, our only true salvation.

AFTER THOUGHT

There will be a time in the future when this time we live in will be considered the "dark ages" of human consciousness.

www.ingramcontent.com/pod-product-compliance
Lightning Source LLC
Chambersburg PA
CBHW041550120626
46551CB00002B/168